Philip Glass

Melodies
for Saxophone

Chester Music

Philip Glass

Born in Baltimore on 31 January 1937, Philip Glass discovered music in his father's shop. In addition to his radio business, Ben Glass carried a stock of records which he often played to his three children, notably the lines which he found sold less well. From these, the future composer rapidly became familiar with Beethoven quartets, Schubert sonatas and Shostakovich symphonies. Not until he was in his late teens did Philip begin to encounter more conventional classics.

He started on the violin at the age of 6 and took up the flute when he was 8. During his second year at high school, he applied for admission to the University of Chicago, was accepted and majored in mathematics and philosophy, during his spare time practising the piano and composing, taking as models the works of such composers as Ives and Webern.

At 19, he graduated from Chicago, determined to become a composer, moved to New York, and attended the Juilliard School. By then he had abandoned the 12-note techniques he had been using in Chicago, preferring the music of American composers like Copland and Schuman.

By the time he was 23, Glass had studied with Vincent Persichetti, Darius Milhaud, and William Bergsma. Having rejected serialism, he was drawn to the work of mavericks like Henry Cowell, Ives, Moondog, Harry Partch and Virgil Thomson. He moved to Paris, where he studied for two years with Nadia Boulanger.

While there, he was employed by a film maker to transcribe the music of sitar player Ravi Shankar into notation readable to European musicians. In the process, Glass discovered the techniques of Indian music and promptly renounced his previous output. After researching music in North Africa, India and the Himalayas, he began applying non-Western techniques to his own work.

By 1974, he had composed a large collection of pieces, some for use by the theatre company Mabou Mines – of which Glass was a co-founder – but mainly for his own performing group, the Philip Glass Ensemble. This period culminated in the 3-hour *Music in 12 Parts* and, in 1976, the 4½-hour Philip Glass/Robert Wilson opera *Einstein on the Beach*, now considered a landmark of twentieth century music theatre.

Glass's output since *Einstein* has ranged from opera, film scores and dance to various unclassifiable theatre pieces. In addition, he has produced large-scale work for chorus and orchestra, symphonies, has collaborated with David Bowie and based pieces on films by Jean Cocteau.

The thirteen 'Melodies' for saxophone solo were written in 1995 for the Jean Genet play *Prisoner of Love*, directed by Joanne Akalaitas for the New York Theater Workshop.

Melodies for Saxophone

No. 1

Philip Glass

rev. 15/08/07

2

No. 2

No. 3

No. 4

No. 5

No. 6

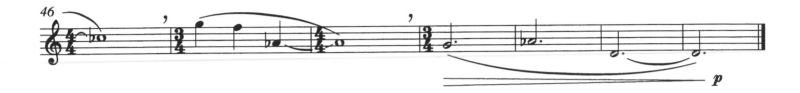

No. 7

♩ = 176

D.C.

D.S.

D.C., with repeats

No. 8

No. 9

then repeat 1 , 2 **and** 3 **with D.C.**

No. 10

No. 11

No. 12

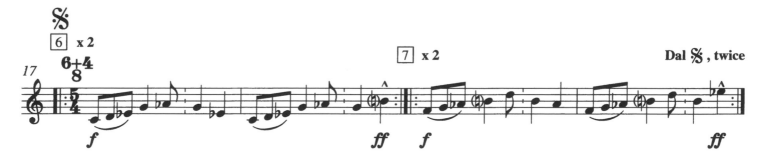

then repeat 3 , 4 and 5

then repeat 3 , 4 and 5

No. 13